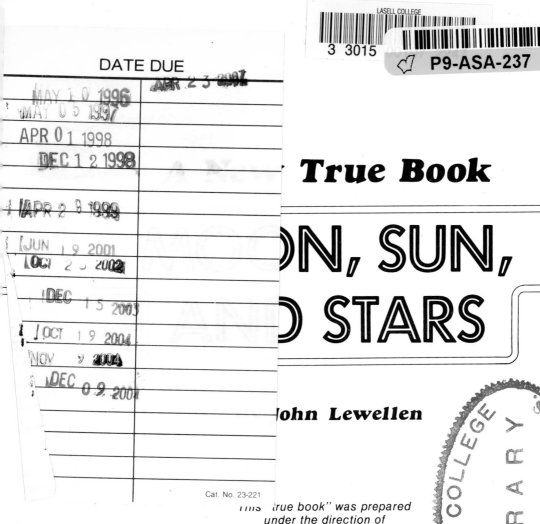

A New True Book

MOON, SUN, AND STARS

John Lewellen

This "true book" was prepared
under the direction of
Illa Podendorf,
formerly with the Laboratory School,
University of Chicago

CHILDRENS PRESS™

CHICAGO

PHOTO CREDITS

Candee & Associates—2, 4, 16

James P. Rowan—42 (top and bottom)

Reinhard Brucker—24

Art Thoma—34

NASA: National Aeronautics and Space
Administration—8, 10, 12, 13, 15, 21, 23,
26, 28, 39 (bottom), 44, Cover

NASA: Jet Propulsion Laboratory—37, 38,
39 (top)

Len Meents—7, 18, 19, 32, 35, 36

Texas State Department of Highways
and Public Transportation—31

FAA: Federal Aviation Administration,
Great Lakes Public Affairs Office—43

United States Naval Observatory—40

Cover—Apollo 12 view of solar eclipse

Library of Congress Cataloging in Publication Data

Lewellen, John Bryan, 1910-
    Moon, sun, and stars.

    (A New true book)
    Previously published as: The true book of moon,
sun, and stars. 1954.
    SUMMARY: A brief introduction to astronomy, with
emphasis on the relationship between the moon, the
earth, and the sun.
    1. Astronomy—Juvenile literature. [1. Astron-
omy] I. Title.
QB46.L59 1981   523.2   81-7749
    ISBN 0-516-01637-7

        14 15 16 17 18 19 20 R 99 98 97 96 95 94

TABLE OF CONTENTS

The moon is about 238,857 miles away from Earth.

THE MOON

When you look at the moon at night, it plays a trick on you. The moon looks bigger than the stars. But it isn't.

The moon is much smaller than the stars. It is much smaller than the sun. It is much smaller than Earth.

The moon is much closer to Earth than any star. It is closer than the sun. That is why it looks so big.

Hold a penny close to your eye. It looks big.

Look at a penny across the room. It looks small.

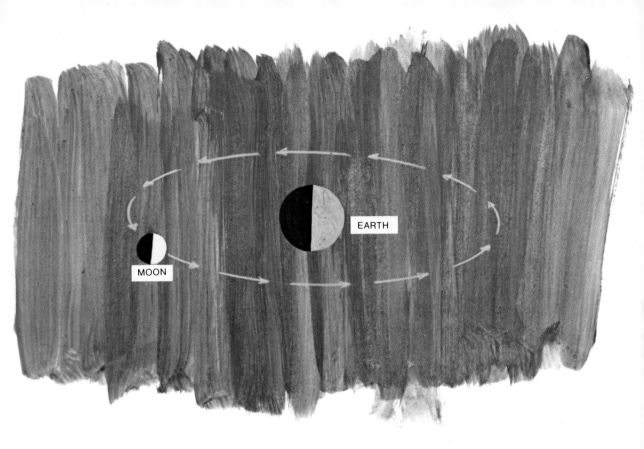

HOW THE MOON MOVES

The moon moves around
the Earth. It makes one
trip in about four weeks.

Craters on the far side of the moon

The crew of the *Apollo XVII* took this picture of the moon.

Days and nights on the moon are two weeks long. Days are very hot. Nights are very cold.

If there were rivers on the moon, they would boil in the daytime. They would freeze every night.

There are no plants or animals living on the moon.

Only astronauts have walked on the moon. To protect their
bodies from the heat and the cold they must wear space suits.
They carry their own supply of air, too.

16

THE MOON IS LIKE A MIRROR

People once thought the moon had fires on it. They thought the fires made it bright.

Now we know the moon is like a mirror. It gets its light from the sun.

We see only that part of the moon lighted by the sun.

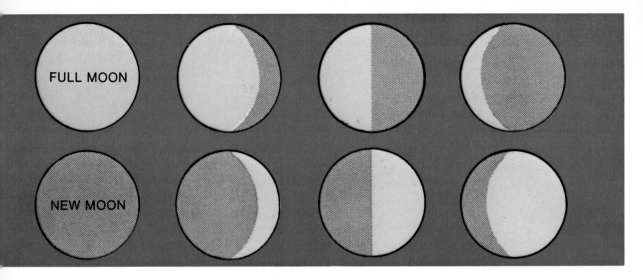

FULL MOON

NEW MOON

When the moon is fully in the light of the sun it is called a full moon. As the moon moves around Earth more and more of its surface is not lighted by the sun. When all of the moon's surface is without light from the sun it is called a new moon.

The rest of the moon is there, but most of the time it is too dark to be seen. That is why the moon seems to change its shape during the month.

You can see how this works with a ball.

18

Let the ball be the
moon. Let your head be
the Earth. Let the light be
the sun. Turn around with
the ball. Do you see the
shapes of the moon?

The ball also shows why we see only one side of the moon. As you turned with the ball, you saw the same side of the ball all the way around.

The moon turns around once while going around the Earth. The ball did the same thing. That is why we see only one side from Earth.

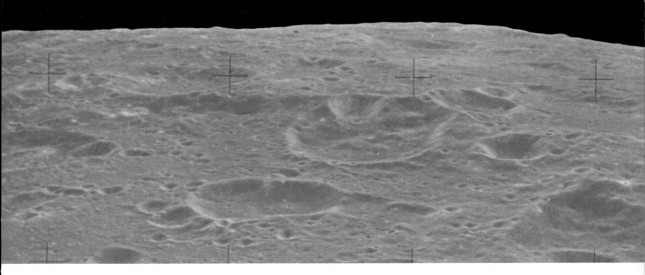

If you lived on the moon you would see the Earth rise every
day. This photograph of "Earth-rise" was taken by the *Apollo XII* spacecraft.

THE EARTH IS LIKE
A MIRROR, TOO

Spacemen on the moon
could see Earth.

The Earth is like a mirror, too. It looked bright when the sun was shining on it. It looked like the moon, but bigger.

The light of the moon comes from the sun. Our daylight comes from the sun, too.

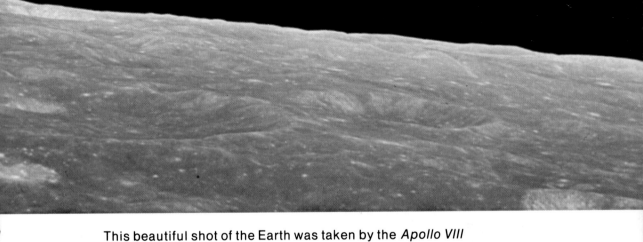

This beautiful shot of the Earth was taken by the *Apollo VIII* spacecraft. The South Pole is in the white area on the left. North America and South America are covered by clouds.

Sunrise in Utah

THE SUN

What is the sun? The sun is a star. All the stars we can see have their own light.

There are many big stars we cannot see. The light has burned out on some stars. Other stars are still bright, but they are so far away we cannot see them.

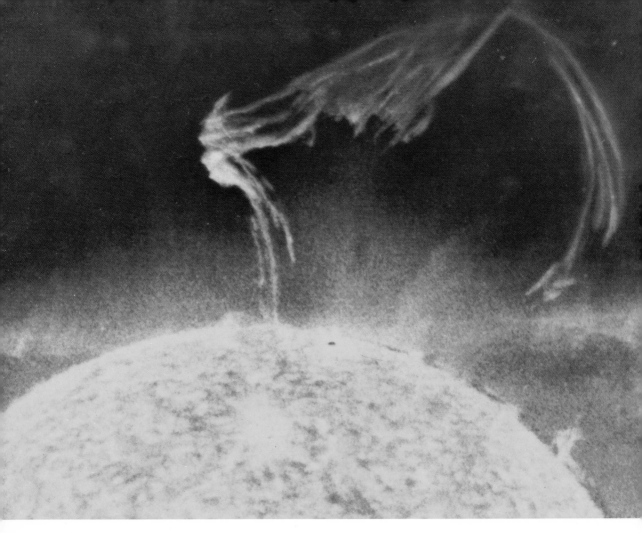

The sun is a burning star.

The sun looks bigger
than other stars because it
is closer to Earth.

The sun and other stars we see are very hot. They are like great balls of fire.

The sun is far away. And the air around Earth saves us from the heat of the sun. The air keeps Earth from getting as hot as the moon.

Milky Way
Galaxy

Many stars are in the sky all day. But they are far away.

The sun is closer and its light is much brighter. It is so bright we cannot see the other stars in the daytime.

Part of the time the moon is in the daytime sky, too.

Sometimes it is bright enough to see during the day.

Although the sun is a star, we do not see it at night. At night the sun shines on the other side of the Earth.

If you took a jet at night and flew to the other side of the Earth, you would see the sun.

It would be day there. It would be night here.

Do you know why this happens?

THE EARTH MOVES

Have you ever seen the sun set? It looks like the sun moves down in the sky. But the sun does not move when it sets.

The Earth moves!

As the Earth turns, it looks as if the sun were setting.

When the Earth turns far enough, we cannot see the sun. Then we say it is night.

VIEW FROM SPACE ABOVE NORTH POLE

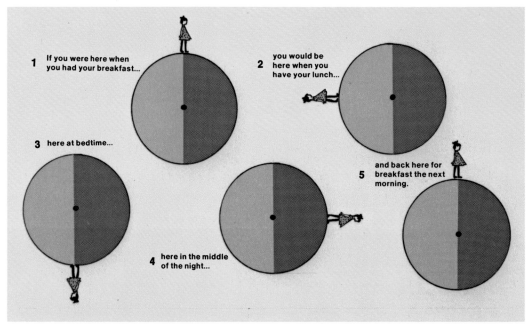

1 If you were here when you had your breakfast...

2 you would be here when you have your lunch...

3 here at bedtime...

4 here in the middle of the night...

5 and back here for breakfast the next morning.

When the Earth turns
and we can see the sun, it
is morning.

The Earth turns all the
way around once in one
day and one night.

You turn with the Earth,
but you do not fall off. The
Earth pulls you to it. This
pull is called gravity.

Because of gravity we
never feel upside down.
"Down" points to the
middle of the Earth. Your
feet point down.

You do not feel yourself move as the Earth turns. That is because the air and everything around you turns with you.

The Earth turns as fast as most jets fly.

Some jets (like the Snowbirds) can match the Earth's turning speed — over 1,000 miles per hour!

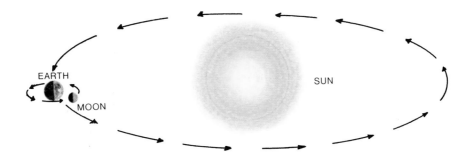

The Earth goes even faster in another way. It moves around the sun. The Earth takes the moon with it as it moves around the sun.

It takes Earth one year to go around the sun.

EARTH IS A PLANET

Because the Earth goes around the sun, the Earth is called a "planet." There are at least eight other planets that go around the sun, too. The nine planets are like one big family in the sky.

MERCURY

VENUS

EARTH

MARS

JUPITER

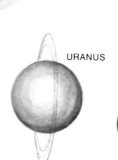

SATURN

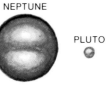

URANUS

NEPTUNE

PLUTO

Saturn, photographed by *Voyager I* from 11 million miles away.

The other planets shine
with the sun's light, just as
the Earth and the moon
do.

From Earth the planets
look like stars in the sky.
But stars twinkle. Planets
do not.

Jupiter, photographed by *Voyager I* from 17.5 million miles away.

Two planets, Venus and Mars, sometimes can be seen in the daytime.

At times stars and planets seem to have points on them. That is because we are looking at them through the air around the Earth.

Venus, photographed by *Mariner X* from 450,000 miles away.

Photographs of the red rock boulders on the surface of Mars were taken by *Viking II* which landed on Mars in 1976.

Stars in the Milky Way. Do you see the streak of light in the
middle of the picture? This streak was made by a man-made
satellite, *Echo I.* As it raced through space it heated up.
The heat made it glow. It looked like a "shooting star".

"SHOOTING STARS"

A "shooting star" is not a real star. It is a bit of rock or stardust falling through space. It burns bright with the heat it makes as it passes through the air around the Earth.

WE NEED THE SUN, MOON, AND STARS

The sun gives us light and warmth. It helps plants grow and makes leaves green. The sun draws up water into clouds so it can rain again.

INDEX

About the Author

Born in Gaston, Indiana, John Lewellen had a varied career in the communications field. He had been a newspaper reporter, author, and managing director for several radio and television programs. His lively interest in many things and rare talent for making a difficult subject easy to understand made his children's books very popular with young readers.